BASIC PRINCIPLES OF EXPERTISE:

STOP WORRYING ABOUT PEOPLES' THOUGHTS OF YOU

Michael E. Garret

TABLE OF CONTENTS

INTRODUCTION

Do Less Worrying

Our lives are filled with cases when we worry about what other people think of us, and the results are disastrous. We play it safe and little when we allow this solicitude to take over because we are spooked by what might happen if we admit review. We give in to other people's opinions when we're brazened with opposition. blessing is what we trade for authenticity. We want to please, not to provoke. Rather than pursuing our own pretensions, we pursue others' expedients. Still, effects do not have to be this way.

We spend a lot of time worrying about things that we don't care about later. One might think, but for me it is important and important now. However, there are two reasons why you shouldn't do this: first, worrying is counterproductive, and second, worrying about what others think of you is not good for you. Worrying is the most impractical use of energy. There has never been a time when worrying about whether someone wants you, gives you a job, or wants to be your life partner has helped you get what you want.Not only does this not solve your problems, it usually leads to anxiety and feelings of being overwhelmed. When things get out of our control, like when we meet people for the first time, we worry. Our minds are programmed for negativity – it is an evolving tool designed to protect us. But today this process is of no use to us. We won't encounter a bear at the party tonight that could kill us, but our bodies react as if it will.Like anything that doesn't serve us, worries can serve as an indicator of where we need to look deeper within ourselves.

One of the most telling signs that you do not feel whole without other people's approval is worrying about what other people think of you. You're trying to find something you can only fill by seeking outside of yourself. You can never feel entire again, no matter how much validation you receive from others. You will receive it once and then require it again. It's a self-destructive loop that becomes addicted. When we care more about how we are perceived by others than how we are perceived by ourselves, we weaken ourselves. Usually, we can't achieve what we want or be who we really are if we worry too much about what others think of us. You worry too much about what others think about everything from what you order at a restaurant to what you wear. Sometimes you lose sight of your likes and dislikes and your ability to have fun and be yourself.

You cease caring whether other people like you when you are genuinely happy with who you are. As opposed to seeking after an ideal that your creative mind has invoked, you have the right to carry on with your life for yourself. You reserve the option to understand your own self and present that astonishing self to the world. Rather than turning into the individual you are endeavoring to be, you ought to be encircled by individuals who love and regard you for what your identity is.

You make up stories about yourself that are regularly false when you invest a great deal of energy stressing over how others see you. We should have the option to perceive ourselves, love ourselves for what our identity is, and afterward pursue new choices to change.

Information contained in this book will assist us with focusing on the world inside us instead of the rest of the world. It fills in as a significant - requested wake - up call that when we carry on with life as per others' standards as opposed to our own, we're living it based on their conditions.

CHAPTER ONE

The Notion of "Fear of People's Opinion"

In the current world, our fear of other people's opinions have grown to be an unreasonable and counterproductive preoccupation with detrimental ramifications that go well beyond performance. For many, fear of other people's opinions ("Fear of People's Opinions") has really turned into an obsession and addiction. When it comes to their parents, friends, coworkers, neighbors, or Facebook acquaintances, worries about what they might say about themselves have paralyzed every human being in the world. Fear of People's Opinions is a method that promotes interpersonal connection and helps people avoid rejection by activating their bodies, minds, and spirits. It's a proactive measure to improve interpersonal acceptance and prevent rejection.

Your visions and dreams are uniquely yours. Only you possess it and can see it. That's a vision that only you can see. Be brave enough to face your fear of what other people may think and take action if you want to succeed. There are some indicators that you could be experiencing fear of people's opinions;

• *You are hesitant to express your true feelings or opinions.*
• *Thinking all the time that others are angry with you when in reality they aren't*
• *You act against your better judgment and later come to regret it.*
• *You may be too afraid to try anything new or find it difficult to change.*
• *The deliberate avoidance of some people, mostly out of fear that they are not truly your type.*
• *You follow orders from others and struggle with decision-making.*

You will damage your potential if you begin to lose sight of what makes you unique, such as your skills, values, and beliefs, and instead start to fit in with what other people may or may not think. You'll begin to take precautions out of fear for what may occur if the criticism is received poorly. You'll worry about being disregarded or mocked. When faced with opposition, you will give up your position. When you have no influence over the result, you won't raise your hand. Because you won't believe you're qualified, you won't apply for that promotion.

Regretfully, because our brains are outdated, "Fear of People's Opinions" is a natural aspect of being human. Our predecessors were smart and wary because they were driven by a need for social acceptance; thousands of years ago, you might risk losing your position in the tribe if you were held accountable for a hunt gone bad. Our capacity to pursue the lives we want to build is undermined by the need to fit in and the crippling dread of being hated.

To live above this fear of people's opinions, you will need to develop a stronger sense of self-awareness. The majority of us go through life knowing roughly who we are, and for most people, that's plenty. We manage. However, you must strengthen and deepen your sense of self if you want to perform at your best and be less afraid of other people's perceptions.

The Fear Factor

Struggle with fear is an unmistakable inclination that can either be a motivation or an obstruction. An essential endurance impulse comes from a characteristic response to vulnerability and hazard. In any case, nowadays, fear habitually hinders our pleasure and achievement, holding us back from going for our objectives. Fortunately dread is something we have some control over and even figure out how to use for our potential benefit.

Fear is an essential human inclination derived from our science. A step by step process for surviving has helped us in deflecting injury and protecting ourselves against risk. The "survival" response, which primes our body to respond to envisioned risks, is set off by dread. Adrenaline is delivered by our body, causing our pulse to rise, breathing to become shallow, and blood to race to our muscles. This reaction upholds our ability to safeguard ourselves or break from hurt.

Finding the wellspring of dread is the initial step to conquering it. Since tension frequently appears to be silly, deciding its cause can be troublesome. In any case, investing energy thinking and pondering my sentiments, thoughts, and activities has given me another point of view. Ask yourself inquiries like: " What am I truly scared of?" furthermore "What circumstances trigger my trepidation?" " Assist me with keeping on track. Looking for proficient assistance from a specialist or guide was one more essential move toward investigating the reasons for my interests."

It's not something we ought to do all alone, and defeating dread is definitely not a simple assignment. It is crucial for encircle ourselves with individuals who can guide and support us and who have confidence in our abilities. Getting help, whether it comes from training, mentorship, or joining a similar gathering, keeps us enlivened and in charge.

Why You Worry About Peoples' Thoughts Of You

When you place so much significance on other people's opinions of you, you cede control to them and let them shape your feelings and self-perception. It resembles giving your life to another person, permitting them to manage your thoughts and conduct. You might not know where to begin or how to quit worrying about other people's opinions since you don't even know why you worry about what others think of you so much.

Your sense of self-worth is low

How did you grow up? Were your parents too harsh on you? Did they just give you something, give you a compliment, or show you love when you did something? Your perception of your own value may be influenced by your upbringing and other life events. Because you prefer other people's opinions to your own, you could only feel appreciated or valued when they tell you so. If you don't think you deserve success, respect, or a move in life, you can have a poor sense of self-worth and will always go to other people for approval and comfort. You may worry so much about what other people think of you if your feeling of value is dependent on them.

You wish to blend in

Desiring to fit in and feel like you belong is a fundamental human need. However, when you make an effort to blend in with other cultures and organizations, you could be curious about what other people think of you. Subsequently, you might be worried about others' thought process of you for different reasons, including dread of dismissal and a longing to fit in.

You care about what others think

Many of us would like not to be negatively perceived by those who are important to us. For instance, you could frequently worry about what other people—such as your parents, bosses, partners, and churchgoers—will think of you. Because you respect their thoughts of you, you could constantly worry about what they might think of the things you do.

Your lack confidence in yourself

Another possible cause for your concern about what other people think of you is a lack of confidence in your own talents and self-worth. You can't expect confidence from others if you don't believe in yourself. It's not difficult to become consumed with worries about whether you can really arrive at your goals and what others will think about you, your endeavors, or your achievements.

Comparing yourself to others

One of the many reasons you could be concerned about what other people think of you is comparison. It doesn't matter how successful you are in life—someone will always seem to have it better than you. When you compare yourself to other people, it might make you feel inadequate or unhappy with your life. When others appear to be enjoying a happy life, you could begin to worry about what other people will think of you when they contrast you with them.

CHAPTER TWO

The Self-Worth Mechanism

The inward feeling that one is deserving of other people's affection and acceptance is known as self-worth. Self-worth is sometimes mistaken for self-esteem, which is based on outside variables like accomplishments and triumphs to determine value and is sometimes erratic, making it difficult for someone to feel deserving.

While it's critical to recognize our areas of strength and improvement, we also need to be able to accept ourselves even in the face of failure or unfulfilled expectations.

At this moment, how would you characterize your own worth?

Consider this:

• *In what terms would you characterize yourself?*

• *How much did you cherish the parts of you that are you?*

• Were the descriptions you provided primarily favorable, impartial, or negative?

• Where did you get the messages about your value?

Low self-worth is defined as having a generally unfavorable view of oneself, critically assessing oneself, and assigning a low value to oneself overall. Individuals who have poor self-esteem frequently criticize their skills and talents, ignore praise or good traits, and dwell on their flaws, what they didn't accomplish, or what other people appear to have or do. Low self-worth can occasionally be the consequence of traumatic childhood events that instill in a kid the belief that they are unworthy, a belief that follows the child into adulthood. Various people may experience this low self-worth in different ways.

Our relationships, jobs, and health may all benefit from having a positive sense of self-worth. Even individuals who are extremely successful, nevertheless, may find it difficult at times.

Strong self-worth may benefit you in a lot of areas of life. You could be more inclined to ask for what you want, complete tasks, and maintain wholesome relationships if you think you deserve good things regardless of the situation. The benefits of having a strong self-esteem might include the following.

Knowing Your Self-Worth

"Know your self-worth" is to understand what to prioritize in life, as well as recognizing and appreciating who you are and loving and caring enough for your inner self, your soul, without "selling out" for material gain. The idea of "knowing our worth" refers to the common knowledge that each and every one of us is valuable, even though some of us are unaware of it. Those of us who are unaware of our value may think —consciously or unconsciously— that we are unworthy.

Notwithstanding, believing that we are undeserving could adversely affect our encounters, considerations, sentiments, and conduct. Happiness and overall well being depend critically on your ability to recognize your value and maintain the belief that you are deserving. So let's do some investigation to find out more about improving our self-awareness.

Understanding your self-worth is a highly personal matter that isn't really related to other people. It's your own gauge of your worth independent of what other people may say or think of you. Also, it has an impact on all facets of your life and serves as an insurance policy for your mental health. Low self-worth causes us to question our skills. It keeps us from having the willpower to pursue our lofty objectives. A low quality of life may result from all of this.

Knowing your self-worth allows you to have trust in both your judgment and yourself. You can move swiftly and take advantage of chances as they arise since you don't doubt yourself and you have greater confidence. You'll be able to recognize the terrible people who attempt to bring you down thanks to your increased sense of self-worth. When you realize you don't have to give up in this circumstance, you are better prepared to cope with them. That's because, despite what they may attempt to convince you of, you are aware of your actual self-worth.

Improving Your Self-Worth

There could be a couple of things you can do to upgrade your view of yourself on the off chance that you might want to figure out how to profoundly respect yourself more. You can thrive, work on your psychological well-being, and increment your identity worth by utilizing the accompanying strategies.

Define Your Worth

This entails valuing your abilities and experience as well as realizing your own worth. This may include pricing what your skills are worth in full or performing confidently with coworkers. You can set limits on how much work you take on in order to minimize difficult circumstances and increase the caliber of the jobs you finish.

Employ Affirmations

Affirmations that are positive can be useful tools. Making affirmations positive yet credible to you is one method to utilize them when you're starting from a place of low self-worth. It may feel daunting to persuade yourself that you will get hired, for instance, if you desire a job for which hundreds of others have applied. Alternatively, you may utilize a statement along the lines of "I deserve to have a good job like this, and I'll keep trying until I get one."

Fulfill Your Dreams

According to research, having a purpose in life might enhance mental health. Following your interests may help you improve your self-esteem and strengthen your sense of self, whether they be volunteer work, hobbies, or your place of employment. A person who likes creating, for example, could feel more independent after completing a project. Consider what matters most to you in life and figure out how to pursue those interests.

Recognize and Accept Compliments

When we turn off praises, we frequently minimize our achievements and devalue who we are. Let's say you receive praise for a painting you did. You could focus on its shortcomings rather than viewing it through their perspective. You could concentrate on the hair you drew too long or the eye color you didn't quite get right. If you think you don't deserve the compliment, you could refuse to take it.

You can find that you suddenly see the aspects of the portrait that you did well when you give yourself permission to view the painting from the perspective of the other person. At this point, you could have noticed that you have accurately caught the model's expression or made the lips incredibly expressive.

Do Not Be Critical of Yourself

Sometimes we critique ourselves before anybody else gets a chance because we're so afraid of being criticized. Recall the example of the artwork. No matter how excellent you paint, you may still increase your sense of self-worth by focusing on the positive aspects of who you are and the paintings you've done, even without the opinion of others. Keep in mind that there might be a big difference between self-criticism and identifying areas that need work. One may think of the first as a problem-solving exercise. The second usually has the effect of making you think negatively of yourself.

Recognize Your Own Goodness

When anything goes wrong, you may restore your sense of value by focusing on the good aspects of the circumstance. If you were absent from your child's dancing performance, you may feel like a poor parent. Try to find deeper indicators that you're a good parent rather than basing your parenting style just on that one experience.

<u>***Use "I Am" Cautiously***</u>

Whenever you define yourself negatively, it's more common to place boundaries on yourself when you employ "I am" statements. Try naming the idea or action that's bothering you rather than labeling yourself. An alternative statement to "I am terrible at solving problems" might be "That idea wasn't quite right."

CHAPTER THREE

Stop Worrying About Peoples' Thoughts Of You

Do you ever find yourself worrying about other people's opinions of you all the time? Now is the right time to acknowledge your actual self and deliver yourself from the obligations of outside insistence. The fact is that although other people's perceptions are arbitrary and dynamic, your core values never change. Being concerned with how other people see you may be psychologically draining and impede your own development. Recall that you are not defined by the opinions and expectations of other people. Rather, focus on your objectives, interests, and values. Sincerity creates real bonds and has a magnetic quality.

Never forget that those who matter don't care and people who care won't be bothered. Turn your focus back to loving and discovering who you are. Accept and value your individuality, since it makes you stand out. When you embrace who you are and stop looking for acceptance, your confidence grows. Let go of the stress of attempting to conform to the expectations of others. Your essential value is unaffected by approval from others. You'll have a renewed feeling of freedom once you break free from the cage of other people's perceptions. Keep in mind that the only person you should want to improve upon is the version of yourself that existed yesterday.

Break free from the shackles of constant concern about other people's perceptions. In actuality, people's perceptions are ephemeral, shifting with the seasons and viewpoints like the wind. It would be wiser to devote your attention to fostering your own self rather than attempting to live up to the expectations of others.

Realize that other people's passing opinions do not determine your value. Put your principles and interests front and center rather than looking for approval. Real relationships are drawn to authenticity like a magnet. You will be accepted for who you are by people who really matter, and those who don't are never worth worrying about. Seize your individuality and end the comparison loop. Each individual is an exceptional mosaic of encounters, characteristics, and conventionalities. You release your spirit when you stop trying to fit into other people's expectations of you.

In the greater scheme of things, other people's perspectives are not really important. Turn within, develop self-love, and embrace the path you've taken. When you stop allowing other people's opinions to define your story, confidence grows. Recall that the road that allows you to fully, unabashedly, and truly accept who you are is the most gratifying one.

Give up caring what other people think of you. Rather, utilize that energy to foster a genuine connection with yourself. Acknowledge and esteem your one of a kind characteristics, blemishes, and peculiarities. Living truly enables you and urges others to emulate your example.

People's Opinions Are None Of Your Business

We have been educated to cherish other people's opinions of us from the day we were born. This goes beyond the literal meaning, such as when your parents criticize your job decision or your professors advise you to make a good impression on the field trip. In our social arrangements, it is also subtly suggested. Furthermore, we must constantly engage with the people in the places where we reside. We play sports together, spend leisure time with others, and depend on one another for many aspects of daily life. The way such encounters proceed will be greatly influenced by how others see you.

Most individuals get their feeling of satisfaction and self-worth from how other people see them, which is a result of these elements combined with the basic human need to be accepted. However, there's a serious issue with this. The views of others are beyond your control. For this reason, it's a bad way to validate happiness and one's own value. You become constantly up and down and are unable to experience long-lasting happiness as a result of this lack of control.

What other people think of you does not determine your value; rather, it is a mirror of their own thinking. Accepting this viewpoint frees you from the constraints of conduct driven by approval seeking. Utilize that energy to construct a solid association with yourself that depends on confidence and acknowledgment.

It is possible to be authentic when you put other people's opinions aside. Your choices, values, and objectives ultimately reveal your true self. Embrace the independence that accompanies living life according to your own terms, free from the criticism of those who may not fully understand your route.

When you acknowledge that other people's opinions don't matter to you, you are essentially given the freedom to write your own narrative. Embrace your singularity, pursue decisions that line up with your actual self, and relish the wealth of your uniqueness.

How You Live Your Life Is Your Business

At the end of the day, the essential truth that arises is that your life is your business. This convincing perspective enables you to take responsibility for the story, pursue decisions that are reliable with your qualities, and embrace the adaptability to pick the course of your life. Your life is a painting that you are making. The choices you make and the ways you take are the individual brushstrokes that make up your life's show-stopper. Others' points of view could be clearly, however they are truly foundation clamor in the music of your own excursion.

Embracing the thought that your life is your business permits you to break free from cultural norms. It perceives that tracking down importance, bliss, and joy are very special goals that are autonomous of observing cultural guidelines. You are the person who needs to sort out what your deepest yearnings, aspirations, and self are.

Your reality is a declaration of your independence; it is your business. Assume command over your life, appreciate your distinction, and relish the opportunity to carry on with your life as you see fit, permitting it to truly reflect what your identity is.

You can carry on with a certified, proud, and fair life on the off chance that you take on this perspective. You are at last accountable for making the story of your life, whether you decide to praise your victories or defeat obstacles. It advises you that on the big screen of life, you are the star and author of your own story. It additionally sets you free from the external assumptions and decisions that frequently invade day to day existence. It's an update that cultural assumptions don't need to direct the way in which your life ends up, regardless of whether they exist. All things considered, it prepares you to explore life utilizing your own compass, which comprises your convictions, interests, and desires.

You might carry on with a truly legitimate life when you embrace this mindset. It moves you to esteem your uniqueness, pursue choices that are bona fide to what your identity is, and set before you a way that satisfies your most prominent cravings. Realizing that the manner in which you carry on with your life is your business sets you in a situation to be both the hero and the creator of your story, regardless of what impediments you face or what triumphs you accomplish. It's an appeal to live truly on your conditions and a support of individual strengthening.

Besides, with this idea you assume command over your future. By making a daily existence that matches your character, you assume the job of the modeler of your encounters. While outer powers can introduce valuable open doors and difficulties, the decisions accordingly are important for the changing story of your life. This thought incorporates individual life as well as profession, public activity and otherworldly life. Being liberated from cultural shows that may not reflect you permits you to push ahead, put down stopping points and settle on striking choices.

CHAPTER FOUR

Overcoming "Fear of People's Opinions"

Getting input and guidance from others is a frequent habit while making important life choices in the fast-paced world of today. But it's crucial to overcome the fear of other people's perceptions and remain loyal to oneself. Here are some practical guide capable of helping to overcome "fear of people's opinions";

• ***Self-Awareness and Introspection***: Begin by analyzing your own anxieties and insecurities. Recognize the underlying reasons for your "Fear of People's Opinions" and the fact that everyone has it to some extent. Becoming conscious of oneself is the first step in conquering this phobia.

• ***Develop a Growth Mindset***: Build and develop this kind of mindset by accepting the idea that obstacles and failures are chances for personal development. Instead than worrying about being judged or criticized, place an emphasis on learning and progress. Promote an environment in your company where resilience and ongoing learning are valued.

• ***Create a Supportive Network Around You***: Look for peers, coaches, and mentors who can help you improve both personally and professionally and who can provide constructive criticism. Making connections with others who appreciate honesty and share your values will help you stay committed to overcoming "Fear of People's Opinions".

• ***Practice Vulnerability***: Being vulnerable is a prerequisite for authentic leadership. Be transparent about your battles, mix-ups, and achievements. By being vulnerable, you foster a trusting environment and inspire others to follow suit. Vulnerability encourages creativity and teamwork.

• ***Concentrate on Your Purpose and Values***: Identify your main principles and make sure your behavior reflects them. You become less distracted by other people's views when you lead with purpose. Adhere to your values and allow them to guide your choices.

You Are The Author Of Your Life

A freeing realization dawns on you in the big drama of existence: you are the author of your own life, so stop caring what other people think of you. This deep ideology encourages people to wield their pens courageously while breaking free from the bonds of external affirmation. It is a harmonic combination of creative liberty and emotional resilience.

Being the creator of your own life means negotiating the nuanced terrain of viewpoints. The emphasis on not giving a damn about what other people think is a celebration of individualism rather than a call to apathy. Realizing that opinions from others are arbitrary, fleeting, and often based on partial stories frees you from the need for continuous validation. You make room for genuine self-expression when you let go of the need to please others. Your story no longer follows a screenplay written by society expectations, but rather reflects your beliefs, interests, and objectives. It's a brave statement that your value is independent of fulfilling other people's expectations and an acceptance of your individuality.

There is a road to emotional liberation that involves learning to care less about what other people think. It energizes a critical mental change, moving from looking for endorsement from others to fostering major areas of strength for a self. Self-acknowledgement and confidence become your compass, safeguarding you from likely critical tempests.

Living true to yourself, free from other people's expectations, does not equate to a life without empathy or connection. Rather, it cultivates sincere bonds based on reciprocal regard for personal stories. It creates a pathway to relationships free from the constraints of conformity, where acceptance and understanding thrive. Choosing to ignore other people's ideas does not make one immune to empathy or helpful criticism. It is a deliberate decision to prioritize your inherent worth above transient opinions, and it involves consciously releasing yourself from the burden of approval-seeking behavior. You take on the role of emotional safety watchdog in this place of self-validation, developing a strong inner core that withstands criticism.

Imagine your life as an unwritten manuscript, ready to be filled in by the decisions, encounters, and aspirations you make. You have the creative liberty to create characters, outline storylines, and bring your authentic self to life in your writing. This is an open call to use your writing pen with sincerity and conviction; it's not a story constrained by social norms or other people's opinions.

CONCLUSION

Press The "Stop Button" To Worrying

Press the "stop button" to worry about what others think of you. Those who accept their true selves and stop being bound by the fleeting opinions of others will find freedom. Your value is inherent and distinct; it is not dependent on the views of others. Making a shift in focus from seeking approval to self-discovery promotes sincere relationships and individual development. Accept who you are, since it is the source of your self-assurance and tenacity. The path to true living—where your own approval is the only one that matters—is one of self-acceptance free from the constraints of society. Thus, let go of the burden of criticism from others, spread your wings to embrace your individuality, and fly into a future shaped by your true self. When you open your mind to the limitless possibilities of accepting who you actually are, and shut the book on caring about what other people think, you will have written the most gratifying chapter in the book of self-discovery.

The quest for approval from others fades, like a passing mirage, as one arrives at the oasis of acceptance of oneself. You might accomplish profound self esteem and internal harmony when you let go of your command over others' assessments of you. Your uniqueness transforms into a compass that assists you with exploring the gigantic universe of chances without being pulled internal by the strain of normal practices.

In addition, when you stop attaching your value to other people's perceptions of you, you make room for real relationships. Vulnerability, acceptance of one another, and the joy of unique individuality are the foundations upon which authentic partnerships grow. People who connect with your actual self are drawn to you by your magnetic pull.

In conclusion, when you quit connecting your worth to others' impression of you, you account for genuine connections. Weakness, acknowledgment of each other, and the delight of one of a kind uniqueness are the establishments whereupon genuine organizations develop. Individuals who interface with your genuine self are attracted to you by your attractive force.

Taking everything into account, the decision to quit any pretense of thinking often about others' thought process is one's very own declaration power. It's a call to make a tune that reverberates with your own self and to move to the thump of your own heart. In this way, quit stressing unnecessarily, praise your uniqueness, and move into the material that is your life — a show-stopper made with the brushstrokes of diligence, self esteem, and the unfazed certainty that comes from being genuinely yourself.